1997

SPONSORSHIP, COLLEAGUESHIP AND SERVICE:

A Conversation about the Future of Religious Communities and American Catholic High Schools

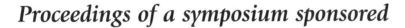

Proceedings of a symposium sponsored

by the Department of Secondary Schools

National Catholic Educational Association

(c) National Catholic Educational Association 1996
ISBN No. 1-55833-179-4

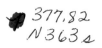

Table of Contents

Introduction

> *I will pour out my Spirit upon all, your sons*
>
> *and your daughters will prophesy, your young*
>
> *will see visions, and your old will dream dreams.*

Acts 2:17

Most Americans do not need to be convinced that there is an important link between religious communities and Catholic education in the United States. From personal experiences and popular culture, Americans see Catholic schools as the creation of dedicated nuns, priests and brothers. If this truth is sometimes tarnished by caricature, it remains fundamentally faithful to the historical reality—the great network of American Catholic educational institutions is in large part the gift of religious communities. Graduates of Catholic schools often describe their educational experiences in terms of important formative relationships with the members of a particular religious community—

Sister encouraged me to apply to the academy, and she convinced me I could do it.

The Brothers were tough, but fair. They never gave up on me.

I'll bet you were educated by the Jesuits too, weren't you?

In recent years, the surprising success of the annual collection to help support retired and aging religious has provided an encouraging measure of the broader Catholic community's gratitude, respect and affection for religious. I am sure that the collection draws much of its vitality from the recollections of powerful, personal relationships between religious and their students in Catholic schools and colleges.

Obviously, the world has changed. It would be difficult (although probably not quite impossible) to find current clones of Bing Crosby and Ingrid Bergman among the thousands of teams of pastors and principals in parish schools today. A generation ago, lay teachers represented only one third of all Catholic school teachers, and filled only the classrooms that could not be staffed by religious; today, about 90 percent of all teachers are lay persons, and there are no areas of school responsibility reserved exclusively for religious. Principals, presidents, deans, campus ministers, all roles once filled exclusively by religious, are now open to and increasingly filled by lay persons, with no slippage in institutional efficacy.

If the transition to predominately lay staffing has been the most visible change in Catholic high schools, changes in governance, often transparent to most members of a school's community, are probably more profound and far reaching in their impact on the future of the schools. Remarkable shifts are taking place in institutional governance, and the institutions at the forefront of these changes are Catholic high schools.

Two caveats are in order. First, Catholic higher education has a long and rich experience with issues of sponsorship and governance, and shares its original parents with the largest sector of Catholic secondary education, the religious community sponsored schools. A case could be made for calling high schools the older sisters and brothers, since many Catholic colleges began as secondary schools, or "colleges" in the European sense of the term, but our present interest is in wisdom rather than age. If Catholic colleges and high schools have some common roots, perhaps they may be able to tap some shared wisdom.

Secondly, it is important to note that lay trusteeship is not an entirely new phenomenon. Lay trusteeship was a common form of governance for some parochial elementary schools in the first half of the nineteenth century. It did not survive the political turmoil of its time, for reasons that are nicely documented in *Parish School*, a recent book by Timothy Walch.[1] So now we know—Russians did not invent baseball, and Catholic high schools did not invent lay trusteeship.

But if Catholic high schools are not alone in searching for governance structures that balance claims of ownership and trusteeship, they are uniquely positioned at this moment in history to provide the leadership, reflection and wisdom that might bring coherence and grace to what could otherwise become a Darwinian scenario.

Although ownership, sponsorship, trusteeship and administrative leadership are distinct and interrelated aspects of governance, the distinctions are less likely to be seen as important when a single religious community takes full responsibility for all these roles. Moved by the promptings of the Spirit (sometimes in the form of apparently non-Spiritual exigencies) religious communities have begun to emphasize collaboration rather than control. Ownership and trusteeship are not the same. In the for-profit sector, the owners of a company, the shareholders, elect a board of directors, and the directors employ managers to run the company and to serve the financial interests of the shareholders. In the non-profit world, owners hold title to the assets of an institution which is guided by a board of trustees. The trustees hold the institution's mission in trust, and employ administrators who are accountable for providing the leadership that carries out the institution's mission. The real world adds layers of complexity that blur the boundaries between for-profit corporations' social and civic responsibilities to a wide range of stakeholders, and non-profit organizations' commitment to the common good. But there are still important differences between directors and trustees, between taxable profits and tax-exempt resources, between markets and ministries. As these issues are worked out in Catholic institutions that were founded, owned and run by religious communities, sponsorship often becomes the bridge between ownership and trusteeship.

A word about service. Beyond any Catholic bias for trinitarian titles, service deserves its privileged place in this conversation precisely because it is the raison d'etre of all Catholic educational institutions and their sponsors. With due deference to the unique charisms of the many religious communities involved in Catholic education, all of us share the conviction that our work serves God and God's people as an integral part of the teaching mission of God's church. To revert to the language of governance, we are called to think carefully, and prayerfully, about stakeholders as well as shareholders. Whatever the civil and canonical laws that define our unique corporate structures, we are part of a larger enterprise that calls us to love and to serve, as best we can, all of God's creation. Particular institutions may serve their communities in unique ways, but all Catholic schools are called to examine the questions of whom they teach, what they teach and how they teach in the context of the Gospel's mandate to teach all nations.

While there are many thoughtful initiatives at work within religious communities and particular dioceses, there has been little or no effort to open the conversation to representatives from a variety of different religious communities and regions. Bridges of various kinds are being built, but there has been little communication among the builders. This is the task we undertook in organizing the symposium on Sponsorship, Colleagueship and Service during the 1995 National Catholic Educational Association (NCEA)'s Convention in Cincinnati, Ohio. It is in some sense precisely the kind of service an organization like NCEA was established to provide. As a membership organization, we can assemble the constituents, set the initial agenda, and provide appropriate facilitation and support. In short, we can get the conversation started, and that is what we did. This publication includes edited versions of major presentations and commentaries. It does not presume to capture the richness of the structured conversations that took place among the participants or the informal exchanges that were set in motion at the symposium. The presenters were invited to stimulate conversation. It is our hope that this publication can serve a similar function, stimulating reflection and conversation about the future of religious communities and Catholic high schools.

I would suffer pangs of conscience if I were to conclude without acknowledging the contributions of my co-conspirators in this venture. While I do indeed believe that the NCEA's department of secondary schools is called to convene key constituencies and to offer them a challenging agenda, the structure, process and extraordinary response to our invitations were shaped by the members of the symposium planning committee. Their colleagueship, sponsorship and service were indispensable to the project, and their generosity an encouraging sign of hope for future collaboration. Our thanks to

Br. Theodore Drahmann, FSC
Director of Education
Christian Brothers Conference
Landover, MD

Marla Yeck, RSM
Director, Institute Education Office
Sisters of Mercy of the Americas
Silver Spring, MD

Anne Dyer, RSCJ
Headmistress
Stone Ridge School of the
  Sacred Heart
Bethesda, MD

Mary Frances Taymans, SND
Assistant Executive Director
NCEA's Department of
  Secondary Schools
Washington, DC

Rev. Carl E. Meirose, SJ
President
Jesuit Secondary Education Association
Washington, DC

As I age gracefully, I find the distinction between substance and form blurs. I choose to believe this is the product of growing wisdom rather than failing eyesight. In any case, countless details were managed by Tracy Hartzler-Toon, without whose support our symposium would not have happened.

The editing of this publication is the contribution of Dale McDonald, PBVM, a woman of many talents who served in her community's leadership for 12 years and who currently directs the Association's public policy research office.

The names of the symposium participants are listed in the appendix. While this text fails to capture their contributions, their participation created the conversation, and their continuing commitment will largely shape the future.

Michael J. Guerra
Executive Director
NCEA's Department of Secondary Schools
April 21, 1996

1. Walch, Timothy. *Parish School: American Catholic Parochial Education from Colonial Times to the Present.* New York: Crossroads Publishing 1996.

As they talked and discussed, Jesus himself

---

drew near and walked along with them.

Luke 24:15

Service

The impact of community sponsored schools on church and society: building on tradition and moving toward new models of collaboration

Speaker:

Most Reverend Thomas Kelly, OP

Respondents:

Rev. Vincent Duminuco, SJ

Dolores Lahr, CSJ

Rev. James Heft, SM

Religious Communities and American Catholic High Schools:
A Vision of Collaboration

**Most Reverend
Thomas Kelly, OP**

Addressing the topic the future of religious communities and American Catholic high schools, I will cover three main areas: 1) a brief historical overview of the contributions that religious orders have made to Catholic education, 2) the challenges facing religious orders in their ministry to Catholic secondary education, and 3) the principle, namely collaboration, that should be guiding our discussion about Catholic secondary education. I will illustrate this principle with a unique approach that has been developed in the Archdiocese of Louisville. I also will offer a few thoughts about sponsorship.

I am not an educator or historian, but as Ordinary to one of the oldest dioceses in the nation, I can offer, through the history of my own diocese, a microcosm of the service of religious communities to the church in the field of secondary education. When the Archdiocese of Louisville was first formed in 1808, as the Diocese of Bardstown, then-Bishop Flaget had three priorities: start a seminary, establish a religious community of women and build a cathedral. The second priority was achieved in 1813, when Catherine Spalding joined two other women to form the first community of the Sisters of Charity of Nazareth, a remarkable group of women who would make great contributions to education and healthcare in Kentucky and throughout the United States. Just a year earlier in 1812, the Sisters of Loretto had planted roots in Kentucky. The Dominicans were the third religious order to begin service in this new frontier. Later in the 1800's, many others came, including the Xaverian Brothers, the Ursuline Sisters, and the Sisters of Mercy. From the 1830s to the 1870s, the Jesuits staffed several seminaries, but did not stay with us in any large number; I think there was some conflict with the Bishop!

In Louisville and elsewhere, both Catholic elementary and secondary education grew tremendously as a direct result of the 1884 Third Plenary Council at Baltimore, when the United States Bishops mandated pastors to build Catholic schools in or near their parishes and established Catholic education as an obligation for Catholic parents. The tradition of Catholic school education extended from elementary schools to secondary schools and frequently on to Catholic colleges. However, it was the growth and contribution of religious communities to Catholic school teaching and administration that allowed Catholic schools to flourish, and in a very real way, endowed their operation with countless hours of "contributed services" on the part of men and women religious.

Today, the Archdiocese of Louisville has one of the largest per capita Catholic school enrollments among dioceses in the country. Catholic school education is a fundamental value of our people and nowhere is that more evident than in people's commitment to the schools they attended, particularly the high schools. It also is reflected in their gratitude to the religious orders that have served them so well. People in Louisville identify themselves by the high school they attended and stories are still told about the religious who staffed them.

In 1995, secondary schools founded by several of the religious orders I've mentioned still continue to educate young women and men in the Commonwealth of Kentucky. The Archdiocese of Louisville has ten secondary schools, which is rather a remarkable number for a diocese of our size. Six of those institutions are private high schools (all but one are run by religious orders of women), three are diocesan high schools and one is a parochial high school. Our secondary schools share the characteristics of Catholic secondary schools everywhere. To quote from the 1985 NCEA report on Catholic secondary education:

> Schools share a common mission, i.e., academic excellence, faith formation, sense of community. They provide programs designed to meet these goals, create a climate which combines caring with order, and admit into their community staff and students who share common values and a common heritage.

Our schools have strong service programs, a disciplined environment and a high rate of academic achievement. Religious owned and sponsored schools also have done a very good job of transmitting the particular charism of the religious order that sponsors the school, even though in all cases in Louisville the schools are staffed by lay teachers and largely lay leadership. The legacy of service that these orders have imparted to their schools is tangible and remarkable. Each is distinctive, but all have made a significant contribution to the leadership we find in our church and in the community at large. Each year, we honor graduates of Catholic education at our salute to Catholic School Alumni Dinner. It is remarkable to me to see the numbers of highly accomplished individuals who have graduated from Catholic schools. These people are making a real difference in our community and, in some cases, in the nation and in the world. Today I think the real question before us is how will the long tradition of distinguished service that religious orders gave to secondary education continue to be realized in the future. The church we now are was formed by religious orders through the education of countless numbers of Catholics. However, the challenges that religious orders, dioceses, indeed the whole church are experiencing today are calling us to look in new directions. With regard to Catholic secondary education, these challenges fall into three categories: 1) the challenges and opportunities facing religious orders, 2) the particular challenges of Catholic secondary education in general, and 3) the climate in which Catholic education exists today.

We are all too familiar with the challenges and opportunities that face religious orders. Our understanding of ministry has broadened and religious orders have greatly diversified their spheres of ministry. Few religious orders have education as their only focus, and some have shifted their mission and focus to areas other than education. Of course, the more negative realities of declining vocations and aging religious populations have caused some orders to seek a newer forms of presence in high schools or to close high schools altogether. Catholic secondary schools themselves are facing formidable challenges, including: Catholic identity, accessibility to poor and minority students, special needs education, just salaries for professionals, deferred maintenance of buildings, and the acquisition of technology for use in education. Finally, the climate in which parents are making choices about education for their children has changed. The moral obligation to send children to school that was established at the Third Plenary Council at Baltimore has been replaced, and it is no longer possible to assume that all or even most Catholic families will choose Catholic schools for the education of their children. There has been a shift in the way parents look at Catholic education; they see it as a choice rather than as an obligation.

As religious order sponsored schools today face unique challenges related to their ownership and sponsorship structures, my contribution to the discussion is going to center around the virtue of collaboration among all secondary schools, whether they are religious order, diocesan or parish sponsored. That is because I am convinced that we can no longer go it alone. Competition works well (most of the time) on the athletic field, but it is counterproductive to what we are trying to achieve in Catholic secondary education. Cooperation is a key element to success, and we must keep experimenting with structures on the local school level and on the diocesan level that will encourage collaboration. We have done some experimenting in Louisville that may shed some light on what has been helpful and what has not.

Let me share with you a brief account of the facts and figures. In the late 1980's and early 1990's, we had ten Catholic high schools competing for about 5,000 students, and that is still the case today. Several of those schools faced significant funding and enrollment problems; others were quite strong. The smaller schools tended to serve a more diverse student population, but were hampered in their ability to offer significant financial assistance and relied more heavily on diocesan financial aid dollars. Some of our larger schools, however, were able to provide significant financial aid dollars. All of the schools were strong academically, all but two were single sex, and the school sizes ranged from 200 to 1,400. The schools were in fierce competition for students. Efforts at collaborative marketing had helped, but did not address the underlying problems of competition and mistrust. Also during this time the Archdiocese had made major commitments to long-range strategic planning, to lifelong formation and to stewardship. Each of these required us to examine the ways in which we were using our resources in educational endeavors.

A task force consisting of educational and civic leaders was formed in 1991 to look at the future of Catholic secondary schools. The final report that was issued by this committee offered a vision of Catholic secondary education and made some very specific and somewhat controversial recommendations in the areas of governance and sponsorship for our high schools. It was the task force's judgment that a leadership vacuum existed on the ownership and governance levels for our Catholic high schools. The lack of clear direction from the top in the areas of system-wide planning and direction made it impossible for individual school boards and administrations to work together to see beyond their individual interests. The temptation, in this type of situation, is to recommend greater diocesan control, but this task force chose a more difficult and complex path. It recommended the creation of parallel ownership, governance and administrative structures for all high schools that would be overseen by a Council of Owners. The task force asked the diocesan education office to play a leadership role in the implementation and daily functioning of this re-structured system of Catholic secondary schools. The report stated

> It is the judgment of the Task Force that the long-standing tradition of Catholic secondary schools in Louisville and their tremendous contribution to the Louisville community must continue. For decades, graduates of Catholic secondary schools have demonstrated a high level of involvement and positive influence on the life in the greater Louisville community. Changing conditions, both within the Catholic church and society, however, force a re-examination of how Catholic secondary schools are owned, governed, administered and financed if that tradition and contribution are to continue.

Following the report of the task force in 1991, each of the high schools, through its owner, determined its appropriate ownership and governance alignment and functions. In some institutions, school boards or boards of directors exercised considerable responsibility. In other schools, boards acted in an advisory capacity, often with low visibility and with minimal designated responsibility. As a result, no system of Catholic secondary schools was in place and this created a perception (often a reality) of competition among the schools, not only for students, but also for professional educators and administrators, as well as with the civic and corporate community. This task force believed that our Catholic secondary schools would flourish only when they began to pool resources, coordinate efforts and speak to the local community in a spirit of harmony about the mission of Catholic secondary school education. One example of this lack of cohesion that we had been made aware of was in the development area. Local corporations and foundations expressed confusion and frustration with the multiple requests they received from each of the high schools for funding and capital projects. Come to us as one body, they said, and your funding requests are likely to be better received.

After much discussion and negotiation among the ten high schools, the recommendations of the task force with regard to governance and administration were realized in what came to be known as the three forums. It was the general task of these three forums to address areas that no one school could tackle alone, including Catholic identity, legislative issues, special education, youth at risk, marketing and substance abuse, to name a few. Each forum was assigned a specific role and responsibility, and continues to function in that role today. All three forums meet three times per year. The Superintendent of Secondary Education facilitates and staffs each of the forums, providing coordination among them. The three forums were divided into:

(1) the Owners/Sponsors Forum which is responsible for developing a shared vision (and specific action steps for implementation of that vision) for Catholic secondary education and to promote collaborative ventures between and among individual Catholic secondary schools. This forum consists of two representatives from each religious order, two representatives from the Archdiocese and the Ordinary.

(2) the Governance Forum which is responsible for discussing policy matters of mutual interest and for developing collaborative policies and procedures for data gathering, marketing, student recruitment and fund raising. This forum consists of two representatives from the board of each high school.

(3) the Principals Forum which addresses trends in education, common in-service opportunities for administrators and identifies joint projects for the high schools to work on as a system.

I'd like to talk now about the successes and challenges facing the forums. The Principals Forum has worked well. The principals share in-servicing on issues like the evaluation of non-teaching staff, sexual harassment, drug abuse education and special needs education. In addition, the principals have worked together to help our education office plan an in-service day for all secondary school personnel. This first unified in-service day was held last fall and was very well received.

Another very successful project that has had input from both the Principals Forum and the Owners Forum is our unified marketing campaign for Catholic education. In fact, I think the NCEA borrowed our theme (Catholic Schools: Excellence You Can Believe In) when they developed their own theme last year, Catholic Schools: Schools You Can Believe In. The Archdiocese provides 72% of the funds, and the ten high schools contribute 28%. (Each school's individual contribution is determined by the school's enrollment.) Since this campaign began in 1992, the diocese has contributed $330,000 and the ten high schools have contributed $129,000 to a mix of advertising vehicles, including television and radio ads, newspaper advertising, outdoor advertising, direct mail and special events. Obviously this is one of the less painful forms of collaboration and is only the tip of the iceberg in terms of what we really need to accomplish, but even this was a major step forward for our diocese. This campaign does provide a very graphic sense of the value of collaboration. As an example, let me share with you one of our newspaper ads.

> When your sights are set this high, achievement is inevitable. When you attend Catholic schools, there's really only one way to go...up. That's because we provide you with a caring and disciplined work environment that encourages you to be your best. For instance, in 1994, 98% of Catholic high school seniors graduated, and 96% went on to further their education. At Catholic schools, excellence is not just something we talk about; it is a way of life. Our research studies continue to underscore the positive beliefs and strong values of Catholic high school students. In 1994, our 1,265 graduates provided 43,779 community service hours and they won 917 scholarships totaling more than $14.4 million. Twenty were national merit finalists; 21 were national merit semi-finalists; 28 were national merit commended and 19 were governor's scholars...

As you can see, the ad is much more powerful because it reports the great statistics from all of the high schools, rather than relying on statistics from one of the schools. All of these efforts, particularly our television ads with graduation hats flying in the air to the music of Handel's Water Music Suite, have become a trademark for Catholic schools in our community.

However, in the marketing arena, there are two areas in which we have not had as much success—and they illustrate some of the serious challenges confronting collaboration among our schools. The first of these is parochialism which has been both the bane and the blessing of our Church in Kentucky. Overcoming it is very difficult. We have to inspire a vision of collaboration among all, including parents, staff and students, which often seems like swimming upstream against the loyalties that have developed over a long period of time. The second challenge is recognizing and dealing with the systemic problems. In the Archdiocese of Louisville, one of these concerns is the small pool of students and the number of high schools available to serve that pool.

Two examples from the Governance Forum illustrate these challenges. The board structures at our high schools are quite different; some are very sophisticated while others have very little input into the real issues facing the schools. In addition, the outlook of the board members has been more parochial than that in the other two forums. This board's forum members were only concerned about their own school and had difficulty identifying and dealing with areas of common concern. Therefore we have changed the focus of this forum and will be providing them with in-service in the areas of board structure, board functioning and in other educational issues, like technology, etc. We hope gradually to move back to a more seasoned functioning of this group.

The second less successful venture illustrates both challenges. It occurred with one of the first projects the Owners/Sponsors Forum undertook after being formed. The Owners commissioned a task force in 1992 to study the structure of Catholic secondary education in the Archdiocese of Louisville. The 1993 report issued by this task force recommended three secondary school closings, arguing that trying to keep all of the schools open would require a massive investment of human, physical and financial resources. The task force proposed that by making the decision to close schools now, in the context of planning, we may be able to prevent the kind of inevitable, gradual decline that in just a few years could leave the Archdiocese with only a few Catholic high schools, all serving affluent students. As outlined in this report, the inevitable decline scenario would be just as painful, but because it would be market driven, with no consideration given to geographic, economic or cultural diversity; it would also be contrary to the purpose of Catholic schools.

You can imaging the reaction of parents and alumni to suggestions that we close much-beloved schools! Therefore, after a period of public discussion and debate, the Owners/Sponsors Forum elected not to close any schools at this time, partly because of the outcry from alumni, parents and students of the threatened schools. The response to this report revealed our inability to deal with the more painful aspects of real collaboration. In fact, the underlying systemic challenge of maintaining the same number of high schools with the present pool of students remains a problem. It is likely that one or more secondary schools could close, and they will close as result of a survival of the fittest mode. Though we may not have come up with the right answer to this particular study, I do believe that this experience moved us to a new level of discourse. For the first time, the right questions were being asked and a new structure (the three Forums) was in place that could begin to deal with the exceedingly complex challenges facing secondary education. Presently the Owners/Sponsor Forum is dealing with system-wide issues, including Catholic schools funding, in light of the massive investment of human, physical and financial resources that will be necessary to keep all schools open, as well as the recruitment and retention of students.

To summarize, I'd like to share with you four benefits that we have gained from the three forums:

1) A greater appreciation for the common mission and like ministry of Catholic secondary education. This has resulted in a reduction of competition among the schools and better collaboration, especially at the Owner/Sponsor level. The Owners, in particular, talk with each other about major decisions that are going to be made with regard to secondary schools before they make them.

2) A better understanding, particularly on the part of sponsors/owners and principals of the systemic issues in Catholic secondary education. Obviously, we have more work to do with the faculty/staff, par-

ent and alumni levels.

3) A somewhat greater focus on leadership in the Owners Forum. The diocese, in particularly, has become much more involved in Catholic secondary education. This involvement is not always welcome, and decisions are not always popular, but I would rather be criticized for doing something than for sitting still.

4) Better management of the common issues facing Catholic secondary schools, especially in the areas of data management, marketing and in-service.

Before concluding, I want to say a few words about the sponsorship topic that you will be exploring in the next few days. I think religious communities have served Catholic secondary education very well by introducing creative governance structures during this period of transition for both religious communities and Catholic high schools. That structure, of course, is sponsorship which I have seen work very well in our own diocese. As a matter of fact, the Archdiocese of Louisville has followed the lead of the Ursuline Sisters and Xaverian Brothers, both of whom have sponsored schools in our diocese, in writing a sponsorship agreement for one of our diocesan-owned schools. Where I have seen sponsorship work well, several characteristics are present: a strong sense of mission in place at the school, a stable school with a mature board and a timeline that allows for proper planning over several years that avoids crisis-oriented quick fixes. In the best instances, the sense of collaboration between religious and lay has been genuine and strong and has imprinted the lay staff with a very strong sense of the core values of that religious order.

I've tried to cover a lot of ground today. I have moved from a historical treatment of the contributions of religious orders to Catholic secondary education to a discussion of the opportunities and problems that face us all as Catholic secondary schools seeking to collaborate to meet the challenges of the future. For Catholic secondary schools to continue their long tradition of service to our church, society and the world, we must continue this dialogue about real and meaningful ways for Catholic high schools to collaborate in achieving our shared vision of faith and excellence. Our efforts in the Archdiocese of Louisville are just a beginning. Only by working together can we identify the systemic realities facing our schools and become communities of learners; learners who can effectively work together to address these realities and continue the legacy of service begun by our religious communities. How to achieve that balance between the individual strength and identity of a high school and a shared vision and cooperation among all secondary schools is difficult but it is a task worthy of our best minds.

Most Reverend Thomas C. Kelly, OP, is the Archbishop of Louisville, Kentucky. A long-time supporter of Catholic education, he has served as the Chair of the Board of Directors of the National Catholic Educational Association as well as the General Secretary for the National Conference of Catholic Bishops/United States Catholic Conference.

Responses from the Panel

The respondents to Archbishop Kelly's address focused on different aspects of a vision of collaboration. Rev. Vincent Duminuco, SJ, emphasized the consequences of the paradigm shift for the role of laity and the need for attitudinal changes; Dolores Lahr, CSJ, elaborated upon a three-fold model of community-commitment-collaboration; Rev. James Heft, SM focused on creating a hierarchy of need centered on the Catholic identify of a school rather than the particular charisms of a religious order. Salient points of their remarks are excerpted below.

Rev. Vincent Duminuco, SJ

The roots of lay colleagueship in ministry set out by the Vatican Council are theological: all are called to share in the triple charism of Christ to teach, to be a prophet, to speak forth the word of God and to serve in light of our shared baptism. In Catholic education today, lay men and women are invited to share in this ministry at every level, but these attitudinal challenges remain:

a) are religious willing to share responsibility with lay people or do they insist on an employer-employee relationship?

b) are lay teachers and administrators willing to accept apostolic co-responsibility for the integral formation of their students, or do they wish to remain academic professionals?

c) is the Catholic population at large willing to understand and prize such collaboration and ministry as truly Catholic, or do they insist on designating as Catholic only schools staffed in large measure by religious?

In the interests of furthering the discussion about the role of the religious congregation in fostering collaboration with lay colleagues, I would like to offer a few concrete suggestions:

12

1) Offer religious initial and ongoing formation programs which would help them to grow in a cooperative spirit of ministry with laity.

2) Religious need to be much clearer concerning their mission and charism in Catholic education; this must be foremost in hiring lay colleagues, in substantive formation programs for lay colleagues as well as in supervision and evaluation.

3) Those who join the staff of our schools must understand the nature of our schools, their particular emphases and mission and express and actually perform a real contribution to that mission.

4) School mission statements must be realistic, used effectively and be applicable to laity and religious alike.

5) The role of some of the religious in the school may have to shift from central administration to creative roles that can animate colleagues in a pedagogy that bears the stamp of the particular charism of the sponsoring religious order.

6) The Catholic community at large, including parents, alumni, alumnae, friends, benefactors and others need to be educated not only about Vatican II understandings of Church, but also about the many effective formation programs that help to form Catholic school teachers and administrators, both religious and lay.

7) Unless a significant breakthrough occurs whereby the government enables parents, especially poor parents, to exercise the right to choose the type of education they want for their children, we may be facing a serious financial crisis wherein Catholic education will available only to those who can pay hefty fees. Failure to mobilize on this issue is to drift into the trap which Archbishop Kelly describes as the "the inevitable decline scenario, resulting in the survival of the economically fittest without regard to the Catholic goals of geographic, economic and cultural diversity."

Rev. Vincent Duminuco, SJ, is completing his service as the secretary of education for the Society of Jesus and the executive director of the International Center for Jesuit Education in Rome. He has been a teacher and headmaster in Jesuit high schools, an associate professor and lecturer on the university level, an international educational consultant. He holds membership in many national and international professional associations.

Dolores Lahr, CSJ

Religious congregations today need to ask themselves "Who are we called to serve?" And when that question is responded to, take the next steps. Congregations need to look at present resources—personnel, finances, property, assets, and with the declining numbers of religious, ask how to best steward those resources for the future.

While I agree that a collaborative model is probably the best way to go, I would suggest two other components to add to that: community and commitment. By witnessing to a three-fold model of community, commitment and collaboration, we have something very special, very unique, very gospel centered to offer to our society that is desperately seeking some kind of model. What better model for us to have in our system of education than that of committed individuals and committed congregations witnessing community: religious with religious, lay with lay, lay with religious, all united under the very large umbrella of the Church and collaboration.

Collaboration is the most difficult piece. Someone once said to me "It's much easier to collaborate with someone of another religious congregation as long as were are not talking about our schools." When we want to talk about collaborating for something brand new, there is a lot of energy; when we talk about collaborating with our schools, or healthcare ministries, it is another story. Here the difficulties, the questions are on a much deeper level.

Three issues surface when examining reasons why religious congregation find the path of collaboration regarding school quite difficult:

1) Sense of a loss of identity: If schools collaborate, whose identity is going to be maintained; how will students identify with one another; how will alumni respond when their old loyalties are not specific targets of the appeals?

The challenges these questions present to the religious congregations are these: How do we educate alumni, parents and students to a collaborative model they may find totally foreign? How do we educate the wider community to the fact that a coming together of several facilities might serve that community better than a set of smaller entities? How do we convince people that these are goods we are moving toward not a decline or retreat before signaling the final blow?

2) Geographical isolation: How can we collaborate if there is no one else in the area with whom we can work, from whom we can draw support.

3) Rivalry: Another obstacle is a lack of support from within religious congregations for any kind of coming together with "them"— whoever the them might be. Old rivalries between congregations for students, for vocations, etc. may have been acceptable in the past, but should no longer be so. How do we overcome some of these old atti-

tudes within our own congregations? In light of charism, ministry and identity, these attitudes need to be discussed, reflected upon and examined before the broader questions of collaboration in ministry with others can be visited at all.

Dolores Lahr, CSJ, is the associate director of Ministry for the Leadership Conference of Women Religious. She has been a teacher at the elementary and secondary school level and has served as a member of the provincial council of the Sisters of St. Joseph of Chambery.

Rev. James Heft, SM

The Archbishop's attempts to bring some collaboration through the task forces are very important, and I think pretty successful, even though there have been some real hesitations about closings. We have, I think, underestimated immensely, the issues of turf. We have underestimated them totally. We ought to go back to the anthropologist and learn a few things about human nature.

In responding to the speakers before me, there are three points I wish to make:

1) Take the long view against the historical context. We are pressed up against the wall facing what has been described as a paradigm shift, and that is very true, but it is very hard to grasp a paradigm shift because it is so big and everything is moving. It is very hard to grasp it in the sense of this is what it means. If we do not take the long view with a certain degree of patience and ambiguity, then we are not going to be able to pick up on what the signals are that we are receiving in this period of tremendous change.

2) Focus on the fundamentals: The point I want to make for religious congregations is that it seems critically important that in all of our work, we get away from superficial polarizations (academic tenure, religious habits/clothing, etc.) and return to fundamentals of community. Only when we are rooted in the fundamentals and stay at the table can we talk with one another about issues that are often otherwise so polarizing and dividing.

3) Realize that as Catholic educators we share something much deeper than the particular identity of a religious community. In Catholic education there is a hierarchy of needs. The first thing is that we focus clearly on what it means to be Catholic. I think religious orders should somehow be less concerned about what it means to be this or that kind of an order and look fundamentally at being Catholic before being Jesuits, Marianists, Franciscans, etc.

I would like to put out a challenge concerning charism: that we realize we share something much deeper that a particular identity of a religious community. The thing I would plead for is, first and foremost, that we sink our roots in that soil that is deeper than any religious community: the Catholic Church and the Catholic tradition. I wish that focus could be really vital and clear. It would be the ground of collaboration. It would be the ground where we bring together well-to-do Catholics with others of real need. The fact is, if you look at the demographics, there are quite a few wealthy Catholics as never before, but many do not send their children to Catholic schools or universities. Why? It is a question we must face and think about and perhaps answer if we capture a distinct vision of what Catholic education is about.

Rev. James Heft, SM, is provost of the University of Dayton. He has taught English and Religious Studies on the high school level was member of the Religious Studies Department at the University of Dayton. He has served on the Research Board of the CACE division of NCEA and the Board of ACCU. A frequently published author, he sits on the editorial boards of several religious journals.

Michael Guerra, chairperson, opens the symposium as the respondents await Archbishop Kelly's keynote address. (Seated l. to r., Rev. Vincent Duminuco, SJ; Dolores Lahr, CSJ; Most Rev. Thomas Kelly, OP; Rev. James Heft, SM.)

Sponsorship

Emerging models of governance: opportunities and challenges inherent in new structures

Speaker:

Rev. Howard Gray, SJ

Respondents:

Susan Maxwell, RSCJ

Br. Theodore Drahmann, FSC

Robert Stautberg

Religious Communities and Secondary Education:
Opportunities in Sponsorship and Governance

Rev. Howard Gray, SJ

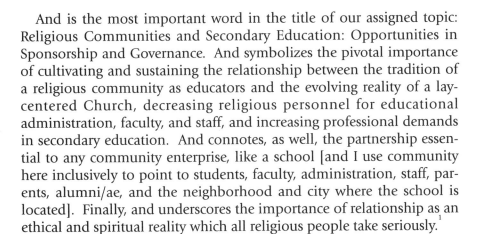

And is the most important word in the title of our assigned topic: Religious Communities and Secondary Education: Opportunities in Sponsorship and Governance. And symbolizes the pivotal importance of cultivating and sustaining the relationship between the tradition of a religious community as educators and the evolving reality of a lay-centered Church, decreasing religious personnel for educational administration, faculty, and staff, and increasing professional demands in secondary education. And connotes, as well, the partnership essential to any community enterprise, like a school [and I use community here inclusively to point to students, faculty, administration, staff, parents, alumni/ae, and the neighborhood and city where the school is located]. Finally, and underscores the importance of relationship as an ethical and spiritual reality which all religious people take seriously.[1]

A genuine relationship must be free, mutual, and oriented towards a greater good. Free because it asks for donation, a giving over of one-self. Mutual because it expects a similar donation from the partner. Directed towards a greater good because it says that together we can be and can do something we could not do alone—and something worth being and doing. While relationships can be defined and protected by juridical bonds, they flourish only in ethical trust and in spiritual growth. It is from this perspective—and out of my own experience as a religious major superior and a member of school boards—that I want to discuss the questions put before us.

A) *What are the opportunities and challenges of emerging governance structures?* First of all, these "emerging governance structures" come out of a history in which religious superiors had made all policy decisions, handled major administrative matters, and were responsible for financial management.[2] In some religious provinces the provincial and his/her council were the legal governing board for the schools within the jurisdiction of the province. In many religious communities which were part of an international governmental structure, there was, as well, oversight by the order's major superior, frequently located in Rome. After Vatican II—not necessarily because of Vatican II—these structures were modified. For example, separate incorporation of the local religious community from the school, the establishment of boards with increasing autonomy and with membership outside the religious community, and—an element too quickly assumed—the development of a new language to describe the partnership between the religious community and the board: e.g., colleagueship, collaboration, or just partnership. Note this evolution—separation, inclusion, and naming, i.e., giving reality to something different.

This evolution was an opportunity for a new relationship. It is a relationship that asks everyone concerned with the well-being of a school to work together to create a community of leadership.[3] Creating a community of leadership says a great deal about meetings, more listening, more arguments, more cooperation. When done well, i.e., when a board works to create itself into a community of leadership, when people are free to express their ideas and dreams, when they allow that same freedom for all board members, when the real needs of a school are faced honestly and together, then board members learn to value being a community of leadership. The board helps, encourages, and expects this same kind of relationship within the school. I want to underscore the importance of a working board that utilizes its variety of gifts to put these at the service of the school. When this happens, new questions emerge; new possibilities form; creative alternatives develop.

But challenges have also appeared. First of all, new board members who are not also members of the sponsor-religious community do not always understand the traditional terminology of religious communities: e.g., apostolate, charism, mission. These new board members frequently have only a vague notion of our histories. Sometimes they have to learn to be "disrespectful" in order to work with us as the fully professional adults they are in every other area of their lives. These are radical problems in communication. And so we religious have come to realize the need for board education if this new partnership is to work. Perhaps a classic example of this need to educate one another is the labor many of us went through to formulate, to explain, and to implement words we used. We have to sift through or own histories to uncover what really makes words we used. We have to sift through our own histories to uncover what really makes "our schools" different. We certainly have to relinquish any assumption that we have the final word—if partnership is to work. From this process, I want to suggest that the major opportunity we now possess is to make governance more Catholic, more reflective of the Church as a communion of the people of God on mission. The major challenge we face is the temptation to give up that struggle and to slide into solely juridical distributions of power which protect our sets of autonomies but enervate or even kill true educational and Christian relationships. And this leads to the next set of questions.

B) *How does/will religious communities' charisms influence governance and policy at the school, provincial, national [international] levels?* The operative word in this question is influence. Let me quote a standard dictionary exposition of the word influence:

> A power indirectly or intangibly affecting a person or course of events;
> a power to sway or affect based on prestige, wealth, ability, or position...
> [as a verb] to have power over; affect to have an effect upon.[4]

If the charisms of religious communities have any power over governance and policy, then it will be the power not of imposition but of affect, of touching the hearts, the imaginations, and the wills of our partners. The beauty of this is that it is the recapitulation of what charisms are supposed to be and to do anyway—to be gifts for the renewal and upbuilding of the Church.[5] My experience has been that board members who are given the opportunity to make a day's retreat, to have some time to consider the vision of a sponsoring religious community, to have access to good presentations of a community's tradition, to meet and to discuss the school's long-term identity with provincials or community leadership—in a word, who are welcomed to enter into the living experience of a charism—these boards' members are "influenced" because religious have shared their foundational values with them. Of course, some board members are not interested in this dimension. When that happens, they risk being left out of the richest ramifications of decision-making, those which touch the school's identity and purpose. Most board members will not want to be left out and so they will either change or stop coming. As religious personnel decrease in the administration and staffing of community-sponsored schools, the process of board inclusion into the experience of the charism of the community is crucial. Note that I used the word inclusion not absorption. We are not asking our board members to become a third order; we are asking them to have a felt appreciation for the distinctively ethico-religious values which animate our schools—in curriculum, in hiring and promotion, in codes of conduct, in service programs, in our school worship and retreats, in our policies on minority recruitment.

It is appropriate for a sponsoring religious community to define the terms of its sponsorship, to harmonize this with its particular network of schools in a province, in the nation, or internationally. It is also appropriate for a religious community to assess how authentic a school is in living out the characteristics of its mission statement and goals. But if partnership is going to work, then genuine responsibility and authority for the school has to be shared. Nonetheless, it is impossible to prescribe or to endorse a single specific legal arrangement which will universally insure the canonical oversight of the school as an apostolic instrument, the specific characteristics of the school as, for example, Mercy or Christian Brother or Jesuit, and the invitation to lay colleagues to full partnership. And this leads to the third set of questions given us this morning.

C) *What are/will be our understanding of sponsorship, trusteeship, ownership?* How are they related conceptually and practically? Let me give this question a context. That context is the kind of governmental structure a school possesses. There are at least seven governmental possibilities.[6]

1) **Advisory Board:** Such a board has responsibility for development of or reaction to policies, but only in a consultative capacity.

2) **Religious superior** [provincial, community president] is the "**Trustee**" and works with a **Board of Management** which has genuine responsibility for policy and the functioning of the school.

3. **Two-Tier Board** in which there are a) **Board of Members,** usually small in size, e.g., six to eight persons, including the provincial/community president or his/her delegate; usually all from the sponsoring religious community. Major responsibility consists in assuring the charism of the institution through a nihil obstat to persons nominated for the Board of Trustees, an annual review of the school especially in light of its apostolic mission, and in extreme cases the power to dissolve the Board of Trustees if it were to act consistently in a manner compromising the apostolic nature of a school. b) The second tier consists of a **Board of Trustees** which is usually larger—perhaps as many as thirty. The major function of this Board is to establish policy for the school as an apostolic institution, to monitor policy implementation, to handle all financial matters, to hire and to fire the Director of the work [president, head mistress] etc.

3) **One-Tier Board** which operates something like this: membership is set at 50% + 1 of the religious sponsoring group, there is a clear legal statement in the bylaws that no change in the apostolic nature, mission, and coherent practices of the school as Catholic/Jesuit/Dominican/Mercy, etc. can occur without a 50% vote of the Board. It make take other specified variations such as 33% + 1 of the religious sponsoring group, with the same provisions as above but with the requirement of a 67% vote of the Board.

4) **Tripartite Agreements.** These involve specific contractual agreements among the school (usually through a Board of Directors), the Province (usually through the major superior or his/her delegate) and the local religious community working in the school. Usually specified in such agreements are: specific responsibilities for each part to the agreements, areas of shared responsibility, as well as obligations to one another, and periodic evaluation.

5) **Franchise Model.** A franchise is authorization granted by a parent organization to a distributor to market the parent corporation's products under strict conditions. These allow the use of the name subject to quality control both of the product and its presentation. The parent organization exercises ongoing supervision to insure that the conditions are met.

6) **Association.** A local association is in charge of management,

policy, planning, and pastoral care in the school. The provincial or community president or his/her delegate is an ex officio member of the Association with no special rights, only moral persuasion. In this model, in an extreme case, the only recourse a Provincial would have if an association policy contradicted the Catholic or religious-order character of the school, would be to withdraw formally sponsorship.

Sponsorship, trusteeship, and ownership will differ in each of these models. However, I think we can suggest some general descriptions:

Sponsorship involves the religious community's overall support of the school as part of its apostolic network. That support can range from simply allowing its name to be used to a commitment of personnel, money, and oversight. It is the willingness to take some responsibility for a school as part of the community's work.

Trusteeship involves the direct oversight of a school regarding policy, hiring of the chief executive officer of the school, control of finances, and the implementation of the mission of the school. Trusteeship is a willingness to take overall responsibility for the school's performance as a distinctive way of intellectual, moral, and religious formation.

Ownership I define as those who can close the school—not merely withdraw personnel or sponsorship but transfer or sell the buildings, equipment, grounds. This is complicated by state laws, but the notion of ultimate financial title is involved.

This discussion is a modest exploration of two crucial realities, both presented far more persuasively in *Catholic Schools and the Common Good*. First, we must confront and work out appropriate governmental structures for our high schools.[7] Second, this mission of Catholic high school education is of "primary importance" because it involves "the quality of the interior life that schools foster in their students, the voices of conscience they nurture or fail to nurture.[8]

Our opportunity is real and exciting for it involves the greatest gift we can give to the next millennium—young minds and hearts alive for the justice, peace, and love of the Kingdom. Our challenge is to do this in a partnership that models, however tentatively, an adult world that reflects something of that Kingdom.

Notes

1. E.g., Margaret A. Farley, RSM, "New Patterns of Relationship: Beginnings of a Moral Revolution," *Theological Studies* 36 [1975], pp.627-646,

2. I am in debt to Vincent Duminuco, SJ, Secretary for Education to the General of the Society of Jesus, and his paper "Subsidiumre Governance Structures of Jesuit Apostolic Institutions," a background study for General Congregation 34; very helpful, too, is Madeline Welch, OSO, "Sponsorship," *Bulletin on Issues of Religious Law* 10 (Summer, 1994).

3. E.g., Anthony S. Bryk, Valerie E. Lee, and Peter B. Holland, *Catholic Schools and the Common Good* [Cambridge: Harvard University Press, 1993], pp. 276-288.

4. *The American Heritage Dictionary*, Second College Edition [Boston: Houghton Mifflin Company, 1985], under influence.

5. A helpful summary of charism is that of Edward J. Malatesta, SJ, in *The New Dictionary of Catholic Spirituality*, edited by Michael Downey [Collegeville: Liturgical Press, 1993], pp. 140-143.

6. I am using the summary provided by Fr. Duminuco for GC34 of the Society of

Jesus.

    7. *Catholic Schools and the Common Good*, pp. 333-336.
    8. Ibid, p. 341.

Rev. Howard Gray, SJ, is director of Tertians for the Society of Jesus, and served in leadership positions in the Society. He was a consultant to the Pontifical Commission on Religious Life in the United States, Religious Life  *Futures Project and member of the Papal Seminary Study team. Fr. Gray taught on the secondary and university levels, was dean of the Weston School of Theology and served on boards of trustees of many Jesuit high schools and colleges. He is a widely published author, and has been a member of the editorial boards of National Catholic Reporter and Human Development.*

Responses
from the Panel

The respondents to Father Gray's presentation drew upon their personal experiences to introduce models of governance and sponsorship which have been effective in defining new institutional relationships in times of transitions. Susan Maxwell, RSCJ described the evolution of the Network of Sacred Heart schools and its focus on integration of the charism and mission of the congregation into the life of the total school community. Br. Theodore Drahmann, FSC, addressed the topic from the perspective of the special charism of the religious congregation as a key factor in the development of shared governance of institutions. Robert Stautberg offered insights into workings of boards of trustees as well as issues concerning the process of transfer of ownership of institutions. Highlights of their remarks are excerpted below.

Susan Maxwell, RSCJ

In responding to Howard Gray's paper, I decided that the most significant thing I could try to do here is to tell a bit of the evolution of the Sacred Heart Network of schools. The Network came about at a very painful time in our history (10 schools closed between 1969 - 1972) and is a real example of the Paschal Mystery. A highly significant decision was made after those closings. Through visionary leadership we recognized that there had to be another way to move forward without closing schools, and that the number of religious could not determine the future of Sacred Heart education. Thus began the Network that linked all five United States province schools and today serves 19 schools in one unified province.

The 1975 document Goals and Criteria of Sacred Heart Schools was derived from congregational chapter documents which related to developing faith, intellectual life, social awareness that compels to action, community building and personal growth. Utilizing the criteria of the goals, the congregation's connection with the schools would be essentially through its charism and mission. The goals criteria were applied to the mission of Sacred Heart schools, allowing for a wide range of implementation that would foster independence but not isolation. In 1978, we began an evaluation of the schools, using teams of lay and religious colleagues under the direction of a Network Commission on Goals. Early on it was evident that schools could not be evaluated according to the goals and criteria unless all involved were given the opportunity to be educated in the charism.

Through the years, we have provided different regional and national gatherings for teachers, administrators, business managers, admissions directors, as well as congregational members and trustees, which focused on unique aspects of the charism and its application to Sacred Heart education. Adults began modeling the values in the goals. The language changed dramatically; people became aware that what we needed to do in education was to surround young people with adults who shared a common philosophy of life, not just a philosophy of education. Presently we see in our service programs parents, faculty and trustee involvement; schools are providing ways for the adults in the community to grow just as much as the young people. In our schools there is a critical mass of both lay and religious, and in some instances only lay people, who are really on fire with the sense of mission; all kinds of people are owning the charism.

I found myself drawn to Howard Gray 's remarks "While relationships can be defined and protected by juridical bonds, they flourish only in ethical trust and spiritual growth." We certainly need to have clear legal agreements, and it is important to keep monitoring them, but I believe that adult education in the mission and charism is the key to the ability to live those agreement with integrity. We have clear reversion clauses with our boards in terms of what happens when a property is no longer a Sacred Heart school. However, there are a whole range of things which must happen before such steps are taken. This process involves our continuing to grow spiritually and intellectually around the value we believe in so that when we have these hard conversations, we are doing so with ethical trust.

Susan Maxwell, RSCJ, is the executive director of the Network of Sacred Heart Schools. She has been a teacher, head of school, member of her provincial council and international consultant on Sacred Heart Education.

Br. Theodore Drahmann, FSC

Howard Gray is right on target in his emphasis on the special charism of a religious community as an important factor in the development of shared governance and I would like to comment on two points: charism and community. I firmly believe that if these two matters are in hand, if the charism has been thoroughly and deeply understood and shared and if a true community has been formed, then the practical details of where you come in tiers, in responsibility and ownership matters can be worked out fairly and easily.

I would like to share two examples from my experience. As a newly appointed superintendent of schools in the early 1970's, I created boards for the five diocesan high schools. Approaching the task pragmatically, I built in provisions for board membership on the part of the religious communities who were represented in the schools. I wanted the religious communities to retain their responsibility for the schools so that personnel would hopefully keep coming. On a deeper level, I also did not want those schools to lose the precious traditions that were brought by the religious which would be helpful in keeping the schools authentic instruments of Catholic faith and moral development. Similarly when I was a college president I "schemed" to keep the Christian Brothers tradition at the forefront of the university. Elements of the charism: mission for faith and moral development, concern for person, concern for social justice issues, accessibility for the poor and disadvantaged, preparation for lay leadership, I was determined to see in the classrooms, on campus and in the board room as a means of preserving a community of leadership.

Father Michael Himes, speaking at the CACE meeting of NCEA, said that we must form in our leadership groups, that is our boards, a community of memory, a community of vision, a community of heart. This is the ideal as we proceed in a spirit of trust to expand the inclusion of laity in the leadership of our high schools. A trustful relationship between the board and the religious community is crucial. A key administrative principle to remember is that articulated in the Holiday Inn motto "no surprises". The board must not surprise administrators and the sponsoring congregation with sudden decisions without consultation and, likewise, important policy decisions by the religious community should not come as a surprise to the board. A practical tip is that attention to fostering such relationships be included in development programs for administrators of the schools and in formation programs for boards as well as sponsoring congregations.

The practical difficulties in the evolution of different models of governance in a secondary school can be mitigated when the charism is understood and the board has this community of heart and understanding. Here the significance of a common understanding of terminology used by religious orders, as mentioned by Father Gray, is important. There is a broader type of terminology which we religious sometimes use and take for granted but our lay colleagues might find puzzling. Recently we Christian Brothers, in a project called "Shared Mission," prepared a page of terms that we understand in the provincial institutes and defined them for our lay colleagues.

A community of understanding will foster a real appreciation of the founding motivation of the order which brought the school into existence and nurtured it for decades. How to retain such institutions as vibrant locales for human and spiritual growth is the formidable challenge facing Catholic education today.

Br. Theodore Drahmann, FSC, is director of education for the Christian Brothers Conference. He has been a teacher and administrator on both the secondary and college levels as well as a superintendent of schools and province education director.

Robert Stautberg

The subject of trusteeship, sponsorship, transfer and transitions excites me because I feel that the way in which we handle these challenges will affect untold thousands of students we will never meet.

Moving toward a fully collaborative and effective governance structure at the board of trustee level is a necessary early step in any transitioning of responsibility and, perhaps, transitioning of ownership. It is an early step, not a first, for in many instances the first steps need to be directed toward promoting a readiness for collaboration. A board needs to be educated to a culture that is prepared to share authority without abdicating responsibility.

Let me share a few thoughts about boards of trustees—used in this context as those who have the actual legal responsibility for governance of the institution; they bear fiduciary and statutory responsibility. Generally, the membership of the board ought to include persons who are gifted in the various significant functions with which the board is going to be concerned. Clearly, this should include the broad areas of mission, academics, finance, legal concerns, facilities management, marketing and development. They must also be able and available to do the work of the board and to be open to a spiritual growth and a joining in the faith community of the board and of the school community.

Governance at trustee level can be challenging because of the uniqueness of situations presented. In some instances a corporate model is applicable and board members will easily apply their experiences of corporate boards. In other situations, particularly with respect to faculty and academics, the corporate model does not apply and it is wrong to try to use it. In these areas the board needs to act in a more collegial education mode. The art and success of a board is in knowing which model applies and how to move from one to another.

The issue of transfer of ownership is a significant one. It is important to remember that sponsorship and ownership may be separated; Howard Gray pointed to models that do such effectively. The transfer I am discussing involves the formation of a new entity, typically a not for profit corporation, which either leases or purchases the school.

28

The transferring or selling congregation can facilitate this process by assisting in the financing of all or part of it while retaining a security interest to secure the obligation and also to provide remedies in the event of default or reversion of the property. Issues with which both the transferring and acquiring groups need to be mindful as they negotiate arrangements are:

1) Developing commitment to the key values consistent with the history and tradition of the congregation; avoidance of elitism.

2) Financial issues: value of the property as well as the years of uncompensated service of the congregation, alternative uses for surplus property, financial viability of the new entity and reasonable limits on tuition increases.

3) Fairness issues: provision for accommodating needs of the congregation for continued use of convent properties, etc., as well as processes for distribution of the scholarship and endowment funds and continuance of equitable salaries for faculty.

4) Level of awareness in the community: need for committed groups of parents, alumni, stockholders to form steering committees and transition committees to evaluate plans and projections and provide alternatives.

Robert Stautberg is the author of Fully Responsible Trusteeship. *He has served on a variety of boards of directors and boards of trustees, including hospitals, museums, colleges, broadcast networks as well as Catholic high schools.*

The presenter, respondents and chairperson for the session on sponsorship and governance include Robert Stautberg; Anne Dyer, RSCJ; Rev. Howard Gray, SJ; Susan Maxwell, RSCJ; and Br. Theodore Drahmann, FSC.

Colleagueship

Colleagueship in newly designed roles and relationships

Speaker:

Joan Magnetti, RSCJ

Respondents:

Yvonne Gelpi

Rev. Joseph O'Connell, SJ

Marla Yeck, RSM

Jean Murphy

Colleagueship and Leadership:
Not Mine, Ours; Not They, We

Joan Magnetti, RSCJ

It is really a singular joy for me to come and address you because you represent schools and religious education programs, seminaries and colleges which stand for certain timeless gospel values. We come here representing places of learning which have shaped the consciousness and consciences of countless adults for whom, hopefully, this nation and our world is a better place because of the particular kind of value system which we have espoused for many years. We come celebrating a tremendous amount of faith and wisdom which we have tried to pass on to those in the next generations.

So, the title for my talk, Not Mine, Ours; Not They, We. I purposely chose that because I am convinced that the true strength of Catholic institutions is directly related to the way in which the original charism and mission are preserved and promoted for future generations. I believe they are transmitted through experiences—the lived experiences of colleagueship and leadership. In a living experience, the charism is not kept in a treasury or a box that we dust off and look at, but is manifested in a sense of how we all together in the institutions re-energize, rediscover and prolong that charism so it does not become a fixed-in-time experience of a foundress in the 1600's that we somehow replicate in the same way today.

Religious communities today are at a crossroads and, therefore, need a new vision of ownership and control. I believe we need a new way of thinking about "not mine, but ours." It is the St. Peter experience of "When you are older someone else will fasten your belt around you and lead you,"—and I will add, "to where you want to go, where you need to go, together, with lay and religious colleagues." I believe that being led well is as important as leading.

The paradigm that I share with you is very similar to the paradigm of many of the religious orders. I share the story of our Network in the hope that some of it may be replicable by you. St. Madeline Sophie

Barat, founded our religious order in 1800, in France, to give glory to the heart of Christ through the work of education. There were difficult days in the beginning of the founding of our religious order; we were a very cloistered group, in fact, very cloistered all the way until the early 1970's. We founded many academies for girls, and whenever we founded academies we were to establish schools for poor children. The tuition of the academy boarders and day pupils financed the free school for the poor, and the religious taught in both of those schools. St. Madeline Sophie believed that when you educate a woman you educate a family, and when you educate a family you educate a civilization. We have maintained that concept through all the changing images of women because we believe that as an international congregation we can in a small way make a change and a shift in civilization.

St. Rose Philippine Duchesne brought the Society to the United States in 1818, when she came to work with the Pottawatamie Indians. She arrived in New Orleans and began opening schools for the "wild girls of the West". It was many years before she finally did get to her Pottawatamie Indians. Among them she was known as the woman who prayed always because she could never learn their language, nor did she ever learn English. It was a very lonely, hard experience for her, but out of that holiness and out of that suffering schools thrived. When she died in 1852, there were eight academies in the United States and she had sent several nuns to Latin America to begin schools.

In our early days, we could not work in parochial schools because we were cloistered and it was almost impossible for us to be out among the parish children and the families. Consequently, our name became synonymous with schools for the wealthy which has been problematic for our religious congregation. We have struggled very hard, as did many religious orders through the 1960's and 1970's, to reshape not only the way in which we live out the charism but how we change our institutions to reflect it. In the midst of all the struggle, the we, which was increasingly not just the religious congregation but laity as well, were saying that we wanted these schools to stand for something different. We did not want them simply caught up in the main stream of independent education, boasting of sending students to prestigious Ivy League schools, without remembering the purpose for which we were running a Sacred Heart school. It was a time when we were coming out of monastic lifestyles, we were closing schools and our colleges were changing very much as were the students they were educating.

We were asked by Vatican II, as were all religious orders, to return to the spirit of founding the charism. In doing so, our schools were greatly impacted and we lost people. We lost some parents and we lost some faculty and we lost some major donors because we began to question our commitment to those children who were not in our schools, but who were in our neighborhoods. We saw that commitment as part of who we are as a religious order.

At the same time we had to make some very practical decisions about competition, cost, academic expectations, financial aid and questions about "are we pricing ourselves out of the market?". Several factors impacted the financial picture: most schools contributed at least ten percent of tuition income to financial aid; the schools were totally separate from the religious order and not financed by the provincial assets; salaries of the religious were comparable with the lay salaries and went directly to the order and without returning to the schools. Therefore we had to develop different ways of funding and supporting our schools.

In addition, a central issue focused on how the Society of the Sacred Heart was to safeguard the integrity of the philosophy identified as Sacred Heart. The goals and criteria developed in the Network Commission on Goals, explained by Susan Maxwell earlier, was the watershed moment when we realized that we had to determine what specifically qualified us as distinctively different. If we can not carry out the criteria, there is no real purpose to say "of the Sacred Heart" on our school sign. We could just be wonderful prep schools for girls that also teach religion. Rather, we have to convey a sense of what we really want to be as lay and religious working together.

We are trying to look at a different educational model. If we all agree that a social awareness that impels to action is central, then we cannot just say that because girls go to volunteer at a local hospital that does it. It does not do it. Students have to understand the economics of soup kitchens and why there is a Stanford and a Greenwich cheek-to-jowl, and how the tax system works, and perhaps sit on the board of directors of the soup kitchen. We have 19 Sacred Heart schools with lay boards of trustees, on which there are a few religious, who really wanted to be a part of this mission. The way in which our religious order has supported the schools financially is to assume all the costs of providing retreats for new trustees, annual meetings of all the heads and all the board chairs. In addition, there are faculty and student exchanges among schools and students have common Network experiences working among the poor in rural areas in the summer.

Every five years, after a very rigorous self-study by the entire school community—faculty, parents, alumnae, board trustees, administrators—there is a Network evaluation by group of five evaluators from other Sacred Heart schools. Through dialogue, they reflect back how they see the mission being carried out and indicate areas for improvement, from which the school establishes an action plan. Theoretically, a school could fail if it did not fulfill the requirements of the Network Commission on Goals. However, we do not let an institution come to that moment. If we are really in collaboration then we have been educating each other well about how the criteria are to be lived out in the school.

A strong key to success lies with our boards of trustees which stand fiscally responsible for the life of the school. They are independent; they interact with other boards for guidance. They rely on the provincial and other religious for ideas and dialogue about where the religious order is going and what is happening or not happening in their school. They realize that responsibility does stop with them. That ownership is what leads to great strength in an institution.

I would like to conclude with a few things that I think we should devote attention to, not just in our Network, but also in other schools similar to ours:

1) Continue to let go in a real philosophic and theological process which evidence a belief that lay colleagues bring as much and sometimes more of the Holy Spirit to the table than we religious do. Be very careful about the "we-they" language.

2) Continue to trust those with whom we work.

3) Continue the dialogue on issues of spirituality and educational vision, particularly with regard to developing the spiritual life of the countless youth who are outside our system. There is great opportunity for schools to form consortiums to address this issue.

4) Continue to let the Network grow—we are going to be welcoming new schools into our Network who are not Sacred Heart schools but who want to be a part of those goals and criteria and they want to add to that dialogue.

5) Continue to identify and train future heads of schools. I have been asked to chair a task force for our Network board of directors on how we find from within our own schools future division heads and heads of schools. That is very important to us because they are the ones, along with many of our alumnae, who have the spirituality and can be brought forward to leadership. The religious order and the individual religious have to begin the process of change with the boards who frequently set having a religious as head of school as their priority.

6) Continue to explore the evolving tradition of the Church on issues of diversity.

7) Continue to explore our responsibility to impact on and be informed by independent education and the mission of the Church. We have to find ways to tell our story so that we can work together with others in independent education who want to share so much of our values as well as the mission of the Church.

8) Continue to resist the models of some congregations to structure institutions so that at least one religious remains, usually as president/director or in charge of mission effectiveness as the voice of the mission. That image does not serve well when we are attempting to promote the concept that there can be Sacred Heart schools fully supportive of living out the goals and criteria with responsible boards of trustees without the presence of any religious.

9) Continue to allow independent school boards to flourish and not try to reclaim our assets. I have heard of congregations which, in an attempt to care for their elderly, are attempting to reclaim some of their transferred assets. Religious communities need to mirror gospel values on these issues.

10) To continue to take special care in the identification, selection

and training of trustees as well as providing for parent and student education to the goals.

Anyone who leads a religiously sponsored school must appropriate the spirituality and mission of the founder. The leader must acquire a vibrant understanding of the mission, be passionate about it and communicate it. One must be fully knowledgeable about the current lived expression of how that religious order lives out the founder's mission as well as how that is lived out in the school. I believe that God does raise up leaders in our institutions, despite all our financial difficulties, enrollment projections, and competition. If we can create a climate of prayer and understanding of charism, people will want to be part of our schools. It is the role of the head to create that climate within the school.

Lastly, as leaders we need to celebrate the little and the big steps of what it means to continue to keep these schools strong. That is what is going to give people the momentum and the energy. I hope that when we all go home we can light a few fires that will truly be a part of continuing this work of Catholic education.

Joan Magnetti, RSCJ, has served as head of school, as well as teacher and academic dean and DRE in various Sacred Heart schools. She has also been a member of several boards of trustees for organizations with civic and diocesan concerns.

Responses from the Panel

In responding to the presentation, the panelists cited examples from their personal experiences which illustrated newly defined roles and relationships in colleagueship. Yvonne Gelpi shared perceptions of changing attitudes toward lay leadership in congregational sponsored schools experienced in her pioneering efforts as a lay administrator. Rev. Joseph O'Connell, SJ, raised questions for religious congregations to consider through his presentation of case studies and reflections on Jesuit corporate identity and its impact on enhancing or detracting from collaboration with lay colleagues. Marla Yeck, RSM, offered insights into the need for reforming and transforming language, practices, systems, priorities and relations with the church. Jean Murphy spoke to the need for engaging the classroom teacher in the process of creating the vision of the school. The essence of their remarks is highlighted in the excerpts which follow.

Yvonne Gelpi

I began my experience of learning, teaching and administration with the Religious of the Sacred Heart. From the age of four and until I was about 50, I was very much a part of the life at Sacred Heart; their mission is my mission, it is so much a part of who I am and what I am that there is not any distinction. In my mind and in my heart it is our mission.

I think of religious communities and their relationship to schools as being in process along a ray. In geometry, a ray has one end point and travels to infinity. Religious congregations, schools, boards, and you administrators are somewhere along the ray as it moves toward infinity. Let me share with you one lay person's perspective of the process.

At first schools close to the end point were administered and staffed completely by religious, but when they became successful and expanded, there was need for some lay teachers. Lay people were seen as necessary evils; one religious order's historical documents used exactly that term.

Vatican II enhanced the role of the laity. It also caused a great upheaval in the Church, in the religious orders, and in the schools. Some of the religious welcomed the change and embraced it; some departed because they could no longer relate or because they sought other options. In the 1970's and 1980's, lay administrators became a necessity as congregations weighed whether to use remaining talented religious in positions of administration or in the classroom.

When a lay person was hired as an administrator, he or she was someone who had come up through the ranks, someone who could be trusted to carry out the mission—maybe. I was the first lay principal in my high school and was asked to take the job as acting principal for a year because there was not a nun available that year but would be the next year. Applying for another head of school position in the late 1980's, I was told, "but we really want a nun." That is what the board wanted for that school. They had a lay headmaster for about eleven years and felt that it was time to have a religious back in charge again, to be sure that the school would stay Sacred Heart.

In 1991, I was asked to be the first lay president of a Christian Brothers school; a woman running an all boys school. This time it was the board that was ready to make the move. Before accepting the position, I did some research to find out what the Christian Brothers were about. I wanted to be sure that what I am as a person, what I valued, would fit with what they were looking for and the direction that they wanted their school to move. I discovered that the seven characteristics of a LaSallian school are similar to the five goals of the Sacred Heart education; different words, different number, different emphasis, but very similar. I think if we looked at each of your religious orders and outlined their philosophies there would be a great deal of similarity. I say this to you religious, not to diminish you and the vision of your founder, but to point out that perhaps many of these values are universal whether you are religious or lay. I am not a unique lay person. There are many in this audience, in your schools who hold the same vision in their hearts. They would not be with you if they did not. They do not need to be bestowed with the mission. It belongs to both of you. They are waiting to be called by you.

Yvonne Gelpi is the CEO and president of De Lasalle High School, New Orleans, Louisiana. As such, she is the first woman chief executive of a Christian Brothers school. She has been a high school teacher, guidance counselor and principal as well as the director of development for the New Orleans Symphony.

Rev. Joseph O'Connell, SJ

On a visit to a Jesuit high school, I asked a student, "Have you had any Jesuit teachers?" He said, "Oh, yes, Father. Very definitely. Actually, my best teachers have been Jesuits." I asked who they were and he named three women and one man who is not a member of the Society of Jesus! The lighter side of this story says a lot about collaboration and the sense of a charism being lived and felt by our students.

In presenting some cases today, I would offer some lived experiences from a Jesuit perspective with the hope they might be helpful in stimulating our thinking and conversation.

The first context: Imagine four schools, among them the following positions will be available: president, principal, campus minister, teacher. Each school already has one community member working part-time on the faculty. There is a young, competent religious capable of meeting the challenges of any one of those positions; as a religious superior where would you most want him or her to serve? And why? Or does it make any difference to you? If you had four religious to assign, would you decide any differently?

My own personal bias is that it is best to build our communities around a common apostolate. I think that even one Jesuit can have quite an impact, but if we cannot have a core of at least three we should probably think of withdrawing Jesuit personnel completely. I think of the word 'attention' when I think of effective Jesuit presence. To whom do we Jesuits choose to attend to in our work, in a school, and with or from what perspective?

Another case I offer as a question: What, if any, should be the corporate mission of this local community to the school? Is this a legitimate question to ask? Is it against collaboration? Oftentimes I do hear other people in our schools say, "We would hate to see the Jesuits going off and meeting by themselves as a community. We are talking about collaboration; we should all be meeting together." What are effective means, if it is desirable, of developing a corporate sense of Jesuits working in a Jesuit high school? If there is such an awareness, what are the signs or practices which give evidence of this kind of bonding? How does Jesuit corporate identity enhance or detract from collaboration with colleagues and ministry?

My third image and case reflects the "Community vs. the Corporate Model". The school has been promoting its educational mission very successfully and it has been doing so with the involvement of faculty, parents and benefactors. Then you hear from faculty and staff, "We are a community until the board puts pressure on the principal and three of our contracts are not renewed; then we are employees of the corporation." That points to the dichotomy between two models, the community and corporation. The religious and apostolic mission of

Jesuit sponsored schools calls people to commitment and collaboration as communities of Ignatian educators. Such a belief evokes expectations of the president, for example, that focus first and foremost on the pastoral role of leadership with respect to both the internal and external school communities. At the same time Jesuit schools also derive their mission from charters of public trust that allow them to function as not-for-profit organizations within a governmental jurisdiction for the purposes of education. The board of trustees and the officers of the corporation are responsible for seeing that the institution fulfills its legal and professional responsibilities. In this context, people's expectations are likely to center on the business or financial, legal and managerial dimensions of organizational leadership that are very much a part of a president's responsibility as chief executive officer. What is considered desirable and appropriate behavior when looking at one aspect of the position, therefore, may not be perceived so strongly from an altogether different angle. How does one handle the stress accompanying attempts to be both pastor and manager?

Lastly, I would propose this case possibility for your reflection. It is called, "Collaboration or Colleagueship May Not be Off the Wall, But is it On the Chart?" Imagine that you are preparing for a Middle States [accrediting agency] visit; you are reviewing the organizational chart as the principal of the school. How does it, or does it not reflect collaboration or colleagueship and leadership? What should be the concentration? What should be the attention of that particular chart?

Rev. Joseph O'Connell, SJ, is the director of the Commission on Research and Development for the Jesuit Secondary Education Association. He has taught high school English and drama and been an adjunct professor on the university level. He has been an educational consultant for the New York Urban League, and has been engaged in a private practice as a consultant on organizational life.

Marla Yeck, RSM

As a response to Sister Joan, I would share five words which are the building blocks on which to create colleagueship and leadership. They are: form, storm, norm, reform and transform. These words assist us in changing the paradigm from mine to ours, from they to us.

1) FORM: As religious communities, we must let go and invite many peoples and groups to walk with us in a multitude of roles, with varying degrees of involvement and commitment. As we form new relationships and partnerships, we must be certain what it is that we are asking of each group. For instance, if we bring together the pastors of

our feeder schools, are we going to ask for their assistance in the liturgical life of the school, in support of recruitment practices, in financial endeavors?

2) STORM: Once we have formed a board, an alumnae group, development committee, we must have conversations on vision, goals, policies and proceedings. We need to brain-storm the many expectations, parameters and directions all of us have for our school. We need to put many issues on the table and determine the strengths, weaknesses, opportunities and threats to each key player or group.

3) NORM: I believe this concept to be critical. All parties involved in the leadership of the school need to identify, articulate, negotiate, and commit to the direction and long-term goals of the school. It is by norming and in the norming that we need to make clear: a) who makes the decisions, b) how decisions are made, c) when decisions are to be made.

4) REFORM: We must reform our language, practices, systems, priorities and our relationship to the Church. In our language we must de-emphasize the religious titles, the hierarchical and religious terminology. We cannot, as our speaker said, speak of those outside of the religious community as if they are an afterthought. Our priorities must change. We must accommodate new ways of organizing. We also need to work at helping reform our practices of the past. We must develop 1) a willingness to modify, 2) local tolerance during times of transition and 3) a sense of humor as we move forward in this reformation.

5) TRANSFORM: We must transform all who are affected by our school. We must transform behaviors, beliefs, attitudes, values, thought patterns for ourselves, our students, parents, and colleagues. We do this because we are about transforming the world. I believe that the Catholic Church, and specifically religious communities, will always be involved in the education of youth for the transformation of culture, education is a major vehicle for curing the ills of our society.

Marla Yeck, RSM, is the director of the Institute Education Office, Sisters of Mercy of the Americas. She has served in various educational capacities in schools and in diocesan offices as the associate superintendent of schools in Detroit and as curriculum director in St. Louis. She has been an adjunct professor on the university level and a speaker at ASCD and NCEA conventions.

Jean Murphy

I am a teacher first, last and always. I am here today to give witness to the fact that we teachers must be included in every step of this journey that is going toward colleagueship, toward shared responsibility. Now, I am not a grand strategist, that is why I am not an administrator; however, I have a Sears-size bag of tactics, and underlying all those tactics is one concept I wish to share with you administrators: you must get your teachers out of their little classrooms, their kingdoms, for a breath of fresh air. You have to give them time to get a different vision to see the whole picture.

I have a little illustrative musical parable about a trumpet player for a musical production, a drama. At each performance he sat in the pit for 45 minutes before playing one note. Puzzled as to why audiences came nightly he said, "Well, I am going to go see this show on my night off. There is obviously something I am missing here". He sat in the audience for 45 minutes listening for his note—and not only did he hear it, but there were elephants and there was an army and Placido Domingo, and Aida! There is a great deal going on that you cannot hear when you are a musician playing in the pit; and when you are a teacher in your classroom there is a great deal of the picture that you simply cannot see.

I offer three suggestions to get your teachers out of their classrooms: other classroom visits; inclusion of faculty on committees traditionally reserved for administration or board members and a mentoring program.

1) Classroom visits in-house: Send your teachers to observe each other, preferably teachers who are not in their discipline. These visits will enhance teachers' mutual respect for one another, will raise the level of faculty room chitchat and will provide an impetus toward extended cross-curriculum programs, which in this multicultural, multiethnic age are becoming more and more important.

2) Standing committees: Standing committees work best when they represent all of your constituencies: administration, faculty, support services, admissions, parent bodies, alumnae, alumni. Such committees serve beyond their task because when teachers sit on one of those committees they hear the concerns of the other constituencies.

Recall Plato's allegory of the cave. Place yourself in an awful shadowy cave with a fire. You struggle up to the top of the cave, and finally get out and are immersed in fresh air and light. Plato then directs you to go back down into the cave. And that is exactly what your teachers will do—go back into the faculty room and dispel those shadows, show the other points of view. It will work wonders; not miracles, but wonders.

3) Mentoring programs. Mentoring programs for leadership, such as the ones that are a part of the Network, as well as programs that are

developed in-house, do work. We have a mentoring program at the Convent of the Sacred Heart in San Francisco where we have the younger and newer teachers meeting with the veteran teachers twice a month, looking again and again at the goals and criteria and educating to a personal active faith in God.

Finally, all of your teachers are by definition leaders. Leader comes from the Latin: education comes from educo, educare. It means to lead out. All of those educators who you have working with you have gifts and talents, and you have the ability to guide them. That is where your next generation of leaders will come.

Jean Murphy is the chair of the Fine Arts Department of the Convent of the Sacred Heart in San Francisco. She has been an elementary and secondary school teacher and choral musical director. She is a professional musical soloist, performing in operas and concerts.

The theme of colleagueship was addressed by Rev. Joseph O'Connell, SJ; Yvonne Gelpi; Joan Magnetti, RSCJ; Rev. Carl Meirose, SJ; Jean Murphy; and Marla Yeck, RSM.

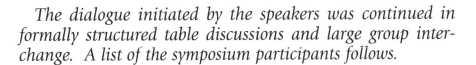

Appendix A: Symposium Participants

The dialogue initiated by the speakers was continued in formally structured table discussions and large group interchange. A list of the symposium participants follows.

Marge Beauvais
Campus Minister
Totino-Grace High School
Fridley, MN

Mary Anne Beiting
Principal
Archbishop Hoban High School
Akron, OH

Br. Donnan Berry, SC
Sponsorship Coordinator
Sacred Heart Brothers
St. Stanislaus College Prep
Bay St. Louis, MS

Ramona Bezner, CdP
Principal
Providence High School
San Antonio, TX

Georgie Blaeser, RSCJ
Member, Provincial Team
Society of the Sacred Heart
St. Louis, MO

Gina Marie Blunck, SND
Principal
Notre Dame Academy Girls HS
Los Angeles, CA

Br. Jerome Bommer, SM
Head of Education
St. Louis Province-Society of Mary
St. Louis, MO

Susan Borgel, CPPS
General Councilor
Sisters of the Most Precious Blood
O'Fallon, MO

Dr. Bernard Bouillette
Headmaster
Loyola Academy
Wilmette, IL

Rene Bourque, RSM
Social Studies Department
Mercy High School
Farmington Hills, MI

Colleen Brady
Director of Sponsorship Ministry
Sinsinawa Dominicans, Inc.
Madison, WI

Mary Anne Brawley, DC
Executive Director
CSAANYS
Troy, NY

Br. Ed Brink, SM
Principal
Chaminade-Julienne High School
Dayton, OH

Michelle Brubaker
Assistant Principal, Academics
Salpointe Catholic HS
Tucson, AZ

Maureen Burke, SND
Principal
Regina High School
South Euclid, OH

Mary Jo Burns
Consultant
Office of Catholic Education
Archdiocese of Chicago
Chicago, IL

Barbara Calamari, OSU
Executive Director
North American Ursuline
Educational Services
New Rochelle, NY

Camille Anne Campbell, OCarm
President/Principal
Mount Carmel Academy
New Orleans, LA

Br. William Campbell, SM
Director of Education
Marianist Provincial Residence
Cupertino, CA

Br. Richard Carey, FMS
Principal
Central Catholic High School
Lawrence, MA

Br. Daniel F. Casey, FSC
Superintendent of Schools
Diocese of Providence
Providence, RI

Br. John W. Casey, CFC
President
Rice High School
New York, NY

Br. Michael Cerreto, CSB
Principal
St. Thomas High School
Houston, TX

Jane Charette
Principal
St. Ursula Academy
Toledo, OH

Dr. Joseph Connell
President
Moreau Catholic High School
Hayward, CA

Br. Brian Davis, CFX
Principal
St. John's Preparatory School
Danvers, MA

Barbara Dawson, RSCJ
Provincial, U.S. Province
Society of the Sacred Heart
St. Louis, MO

Lucille Dean, SP
Principal
Providence High School
Burbank, CA

Rev. Paul Deutsch, SJ
Principal
Jesuit College Preparatory
Dallas, TX

Mary Dolan, SU
Principal
Notre Dame School
New York, NY

Rev. Walter Dolan, OFM
President
Padua Franciscan High School
Parma, OH

Br. Theodore Drahmann, FSC
Director of Education
Christian Brothers Conference
Landover, MD

Rev. Vincent Duminuco, SJ
International Secretary for Jesuit
Education
International Center for Jesuit
Education
Rome ITALY

Mary Cabrini Durkin, OSU
Superior
Ursuline of Cincinnati
Cincinnati, OH

Ann Durst, SHCJ
Trustee
Cornelia Connely School
San Diego, CA

Mary Walter, DuVal, SSND
Principal
Academy of the Holy Angels
Richfield, MN

Anne Dyer, RSCJ
Headmistress
Stone Ridge School of the Sacred
Heart
Bethesda, MD

Loyola Edelen, SBS
Community Leader
Xavier Prep School
New Orleans, LA

Elaine Englert, SSJ
Principal
Bishop Kearney High School
Rochester, NY

Terry Fairholm
CFO
The Suddes Group
Chicago, IL

Dr. Roberta Felker
President, Seton Academy
President, Women's Schools
Together
Seton Academy
South Holland, IL

Rev. James Flynn, OSA
Malvern Preparatory School for
Boys
Malvern, PA

49

Paul Gallagher
Associate Executive Director
Association of Catholic Colleges
and Universities
Washington, DC

Alice Gallin, OSU
Scholar in Residence
The Catholic University of
America
Washington, DC

James Gay
Principal
De La Salle Institute
Chicago, IL

Mary Gehringer, OSM
Assistant Provincial
Servants of Mary
Omaha, NE

Yvonne Gelpi
President and CEO
De La Salle High School
New Orleans, LA

Nannette Gentile, DC
Community Leader
Daughters of Charity of St.
Vincent de Paul
St. Louis, MO

Br. Richard Gilman, CSC
President
Holy Cross College
Notre Dame, IN

Nancy Glass
Teacher and Director of
Curriculum
St. Edward High School
Lakewood, OH

Anne Madeline Godefray, VHM
Superior
Visitation Monastery and
Academy
St. Louis, MO

Mary Ann Governal, OSF
Director of Curriculum
Archdiocese of St. Louis
St. Louis, MO

Matthew Goyette
Principal
Bishop McNamara High School
Forestville, MD

Rev. Howard Gray, SJ
Director of Tertians
University of Detroit-Mercy
Detroit, MI

Marie Paul Grech, SND
Educational Director/Secondary
Coordinator
Sisters of Notre Dame
St. Matthias High School
Huntington Park, CA

Carol Gregory, SND
Principal
Notre Dame Academy
Toledo, OH

Mary Griffin
Public Relations and Recruitment
Seton Academy
South Holland, IL

Michael J. Guerra
Executive Director
Secondary Schools Department
NCEA
Washington, DC

Br. Hank Hammer, FMS
Principal
Marist High School
Chicago, IL

Bernadette Hannaway, OSU
Assistant Provincial
Ursuline-Roman Union
Ursuline Provincialate
Bronx, NY

Pam Harding, CSJ
Associate Principal
St. Joseph Academy
St. Louis, MO

Cecilia Harrington, CSJ
St. Paul, MN

Rev. James Heft, SM
Provost
University of Dayton
Dayton, OH

Dr. Claire Helm
President
Academy of the Holy Names
Tampa, FL

Mary Jane Herb, IHM
Trustee
Everett, MA

Alice Hession
Administration
Mount St. Joseph High School
Baltimore, MD

Rosemary Hocevar, OSU
Vice President for Institutional
Advancement
Ursuline College
Pepper Pike, OH

Br. Cornelius Hubbuch, CFX
Director of Staff Formation
Xaverian Brothers Provincialate
Ellicott City, MD

Br. Stephen LaMendola, CSC
Provincial Counselor
Brothers of the Holy Cross,
Eastern Province
Flushing, NY

Carolyn Lausch
English Teacher
Brebeuf Preparatory School
Indianapolis, IN

Frances Lauretti, MPF
Villa Walsh
Morristown, NJ

Isabelle Lenhardt
Administrator
Visitation Academy
St. Louis, MO

Br. Jerome Lessard, FIC
Walsh University
Canton, OH

Lynn Levo, CSJ
Congregational Leader
Congregational Center
St. Louis, MO

Rev. Vincent Lopez, OP
Principal
Marish High School
Eugene, OR

Joan Magnetti, RSCJ
Headmistress, Convent of the
Sacred Heart
The Cottage Community
Greenwich, CT

Audrey Mahoney, CCVI
General Provincial
San Antonio, TX

Mary C. Marchal, SC
Ministry Coordinator
Sisters of Charity
Mount St. Joseph, OH

Susan Maxwell, RSCJ
Executive Director
Network of Sacred Heart Schools
Newton, MA

Rev. Thomas McClain, SJ
Assistant to Provincial for
Secondary Education
Detroit Province - Society of
Jesus
Detroit, MI

Br. Pat McCloskey, OFM
Chaplain
Roger Bacon High School
Cincinnati, OH

Eileen McDevitt, SHCJ
Educational Director
SHCJ School Network
Drexel Hill, PA

Dale McDonald, PBVM
Past President
Presentation Sisters (New York)
Boston College
Chestnut Hill, MA

Maureen McElroy, RSM
Principal
St. Mary's Academy - Bay View
Riverside, RI

Br. John McGovern, CSC
Assistant Provincial
Brothers of Holy Cross
New Rochelle, NY

Mary Benet McKinney, OSB
Prioress
Benedictine Sisters
Chicago, IL

Rev. Joseph McLaughlin,
O.Praem.
Headmaster
Archmere Academy
Claymont, DE

Colleen McNicholas, OP, PhD
Assistant Dean
School of Education
Rosary College
River Forest, IL

Ted Mechley
Board Chair
St. Ursula Academy
Cincinnati, OH

Elizabeth Meegan, OP
Community Leader
Sinsinawa Dominicans
Sinsinawa, WI

Margaret Mehigan, OP
Coordinator for Sponsorship &
Mission Effectiveness
Adrain Dominican Sisters
Adrian, MI

Rev. Carl E. Meirose, SJ
President
Jesuit Secondary Education
Association
Washington, DC

Rev. Ralph Metts, SJ
JSEA Commission on Research
and Development
Fordham University at Lincoln
Center
New York, NY

Patricia Modenbach
Director of Public Relations
St. Stanislaus College Prep
Bay St. Louis, MS

Br. James Moffett, CFC
Provincial
Congregation of Christian
Brothers
Eastern American Province
New Rochelle, NY

Antoinette Marie Moon, SND
Principal
St. Matthias School
Huntington Park, CA

M. Christopher Moore, CSSF
Principal
Our Lady of the Sacred Heart
Corapolis, PA

Br. Charles Moran, CFX
Director of Education and
Sponsorship
American Northeastern Province
Xaverian Brothers Provincialate
Milton, MA

Br. James Moran
Hales Franciscan High School
Chicago, IL

Margaret Moser, OSU
Principal
Ursuline Academy
Dallas, TX

Dr. Robert Muccigrosso
Principal
Nazareth Regional High School
Brooklyn, NY

David Mueller
Principal
St. Xavier High School
Cincinnati, OH

Br. Frederick Mueller, FSC
Principal
La Salle Academy
Providence, RI

Jean Murphy
Chair, Fine Arts Department
Convent of the Sacred Heart
San Francisco, CA

Br. Lawrence Murphy
All Hallows Institute School
Bronx, NY

Nora Murphy
Assistant Superintendent of
Schools
Archdiocese of New York
New York, NY

Frances Naldony, OP
Community Leader -
Dominicans
Archdiocese of Detroit
Detroit, MI

Rev. Donald Nastold, SJ
Assistant for Secondary
Education
Chicago Province Jesuits
Chicago, IL

Br. William Nick, CSC
President
Notre Dame High School
Sherman Oaks, CA

John S. Nolan
Former Board Chair, Connelly
School of the Holy Child
Miller and Chevalier, Chartered
Washington, DC

Rev. Joseph O'Connell, SJ
Director
JSEA Commission on Research
and Development
Fordham University at Lincoln
Center
New York, NY

Br. Frank O'Donnell, SM
Assistant Provincial for Education
New York Province
Baltimore, MD

Madonna O'Hara, OSU
President
Ursuline Academy
St. Louis, MO

Dr. James O'Leary
Biology/Anatomy Teacher
Seton Academy
South Holland, IL

Br. John Olsen, CFX
Xaverian Brothers Provincialate
Ellicott City, MD

Rev. Ronald Olszewski, OSFS
President
St. Francis de Sales High School
Toledo, OH

John Owen
School Board Member
Diocese of Oakland
Clayton, CA

Paul Owens
Principal
St. Louis University High School
St. Louis, MO

Dr. Lorraine Ozar
Academic Dean for Curriculum
and Instruction
Loyola Academy
Wilmette, IL

Br. John Paige, CSC
President
Bishop McNamara High School
Forestville, MD

Rev. John Pejza, OSA
Province Director of Education
Villanova Preparatory School
Ojai, CA

Donna Pollard, OP
Principal
St. Pius X High School
Houston, TX

Br. Edmond Precourt, FSC
Auxilary Provincial/Director of
Education
De La Salle Christian Brothers -
New England/Long Island
Province
Long Island, NY

Annabelle Raiche, CSJ
Professor of Education
College of St. Catherine
St. Paul, MN

Corinne Raven, RSM
Principal
Mother McAuley High School
Chicago, IL

Dominica Rocchio, SC
Superintendent of Schools
Archdiocese of Newark
Irvington, NJ

Br. Ronald Roggenback, FSC
Director of Education
De La Salle Christian Brothers
San Francisco Province
Napa, CA

Marjorie Rudemiller, RSM
Sponsorship Coordinator - Mercy
Regional Community of
Cincinnati
Cincinnati, OH

Margaret Ryan, OP
Principal
Aquinas High School
Bronx, NY

Very Rev. Bradley Schaeffer, SJ
Provincial
Society of Jesus - Chicago
Province
Chicago, IL

Br. Robert Schieler, FSC
Auxilary Provincial Director of
Education
De La Salle Christian Brothers
Baltimore Province
Adamstown, MD

Carmen Schnyder, CPPS
Board Member
Catholic Education Office
St. Louis, MO

Dr. Elaine Schuster
Superintendent of Schools
Archdiocese of Chicago
Chicago, IL

Rev. Dan Senger, OFM
Teacher
Padua Franciscan High School
Parma, OH

Mary Serra, CSSF
Director of Education Ministries
Felician Sisters
Livonia, MI

Judy Shanahan
General Counsel
Sisters of Providence
St. Mary's of the Woods, IN

Lourdes Sheehan, RSM
Secretary for Education
US Catholic Conference
Washington, DC

Mieko Shinjo, RSCJ
President
Sacred Heart School
Coorporation
Tokyo 150 JAPAN

Br. Thomas Smith, OFM
Campus Minister
Padua Franciscan High School
Parma, OH

Shirley Speaks
Executive Director
Ursuline Academy of Cincinnati
Cincinnati, OH

Br. James Spooner, CSC
President
St. Edward High School
Lakewood, OH

Robert Stautberg
Board Member
Cincinnati, OH

Br. William Stoldt, CFC
President
Iona Preparatory School
New Rochelle, NY

Mary Frances Taymans, SND, EdD
Assistant Executive Director
Secondary Schools Department
NCEA
Washington, DC

Dr. Karen Tichy
Director of Secondary Schools
Archdiocese of St. Louis
St. Louis, MO

Paula Toner, RSCJ
Head of School
Duchesne Academy of the Sacred
Heart
Houston, TX

Mary E. Tracy, SNJM
Principal
Holy Names Academy
Seattle, WA

Michael Trainor
English Teacher
St. Xavier High School
Cincinnati, OH

Deborah Troillette, RSM
Community Leader - Mercy
Regional Community of St.
Louis
St. Louis, MO

Dr. Donald Urbancic
Headmaster
Loyola Blakefield High School
Towson, MD

Sue Villarreal
Faculty Member
Moreau Catholic High School
Hayward, CA

Mary Denise Villaume, VHM
Visitation Monastery
Medota Heights, MN

M. Gervaise Volpey, OP
Head of School
San Domenico School
San Anselmo, CA

Br. Brian Walsh, CFC
Educational Director
Congregation of Christian
Brothers
Eastern American Province
New Rochelle, NY

58

Maureen Welsh, SHCJ
Director, National Testing
Program
College Board
New York, NY

Rev. Ted Wojcicki
Catholic Education Office
Archdiocese of St. Louis
Saint Louis, MO

Marla Yeck, RSM
Director, Institute Education
Office
Sisters of Mercy of the Americas
Silver Spring, MD

Ann Zanders
President
Xavier Prep School
New Orleans, LA

Linda Zechmeister, CPPS
Principal
St. Elizabeth Academy
St. Louis, MO